Joywalks
By Harrison Reed Gross

Joywalks.
Alpha edition.
Copyright 2013 Sphirah Corporation.

Poems written in United States 2012-2013.
Front & back cover, "Griffin Boulevard After Dark,"
by the author.
Author shot courtesy of Ayèlet Pearl.
ISBN-13: 978-0615777504 (Sphirah)
ISBN-10: 0615777503

As a work of art under license to Sphirah for reproduction, this product has a charitable aim, in tandem with its educational or entertainment value. This is accomplished through the special Orlah Contract, which I created as the founding principle of Sphirah to convert the positive momentum of art into a charitable force. For a maximum of the first three years a work of art is contracted to Sphirah, all of the profit it generates goes directly to the artist. After this initial period, the profit on any sale of the work is divided between the artist and any charitable causes of his or her choice. A minimum of one third of all profit on the licensed product is sent directly to the charities after the Orlah Phase. The goal of Sphirah is to harmonize the artist's proliferation with his or her compassion, providing them the opportunity to raise capital for noble causes through their art.

Warm Wishes,
Harrison Reed Gross
Founder and First Chair Poet

Time grows upon the rock.

...W. Stevens

A selection of forty-five poems...

...marching through shades of allusion.

Spearmint Sunrise

The world is one,
in quiet calm.

Them's the breaks,
A storm of a man—
Technique is the tradition.

God draws a soaring dove with a paintbrush.

Dreamliquid, tiptoe—
The palms grow straight and narrow.

Scars don't make the man,
Rolling in shake mode.

Pry open the cold clasp,
Commune with a wasp.

Six spiders spin silk
From my chin to the floor.

A knowing conviction,
A telling faith.

The world was one,
This morning a minty memory.

Trot Through Botanicals

I am hunter-gatherer of æther ashes,
Wintertide ices over my eyelashes.

What is the gash of your glittery design?
Pattern of gulls in the flash of a turbine.

Hot sugar,
corrosive cruster of my counter,
Score and steam in diamond fractals of nighttide.

The time rises nigh, the kettle whistles low,
What was dashing royal
fades to indigo.

Conceptual connection,
imagined interaction.
Exegetical encounter.

My shadow took a knee
in blades of a clearing
and began a cantrip.

Take a sip of imaginary coffee.
Daydream a bogue this time,
And ignite it with your fiery mind.

Let's Get Shakes

Wash in my kingdom,
Wash clean.

My shadow has an eye of his own.

Take the poet out for a think.
Slip into a slow funk,
On one of those long, drink-me-in walks.

My shadow wears a wingtip,
A monkstrap, a cap-toe oxford.

Measure the moon,
Sweep it clean with a yew broom.

My shadow checks his reflection in pavement.

Yesterday was decadent,
Tonight in decay.

Today, the deranged,
Tomorrow, the dead.

I do not know,
My shadow may have said so.
He has a life of his own.

Dandy coyote.
Okay compadre, whatever you say.
Easy gypsy.

He picks Fuji apples
at midnight. My shadow

Strikes a match, and smiles.

Hobbies & habits, droids & drugs.
The night is a hylozoist beast.

He dances like light through a screen—
My shadow kisses doves on the crown
and follows me.

On the Origin of Species

Let me get it started for you.
Another day,
Another dark hollow.

On a rollercoaster lit with jack-o-lanterns,
Rickety minecart above a haunted Victorian.

The sunspot on my eye
looks like a microscope.

Life is cocoa, hot & cold,
Complete control.
I walk naked in capes
In cloaked capers.

A verse is a grinding device.
Some days I am Jekyll,
Sometimes I'm implied.

That moment when you realize
What have I been smoking,
listening to all my life.

My poetry professor
stalked a hooker,
Said it was an exercise.

I won't make excuses
for the rustling past.

ᗡᗞ

A bundle of pines,
Abundant needles.
The evening stinking

of predation & patricians.

I am an entertainer first,
Literate across languages.
Just got the nice.

Murky snakewood,
twin quickthorns.
Hippo ivory.

My professor's pipe puffs
Cherrily before the greengrocery,
With cloudy haplographies,
Hendiates,
To the haberdashery.

Only to ply down a
dead end.

One man. One pen.
One poem.

Everglades, egret.
    Crocodile

Snapping off
more than you can chew.

Somewhere

Many upstarts in this world,
So rare to find a finish.

Somewhere
in the time of Hezekiah,
beautiful things exist tartly
far from my torched treacherous torrent.

I left two fans running all semester
One in my blaze,
And one in my wake.

Just as it will wax
So too will it wane.
An armada of
Portuguese men o' war—

Hymn of Pan, Funeste, Sea Surface...

Doctrinaires unvidiated,
irrefragable desuetude—
Just as it boons, so too does it bane.
Plant the pips and plumstones.

Apply apples. Erysipelas, deep hemorrhagic infarcts'
toxaemia.
Plankter nektic or benthic,
St. Anthony's fire...St. Hubert's key.
Stupid tuber. Nabokovian

Glowing cattle skulls
Desperate for a drink,
Superlatively verisimilar.

Auricula

I'll hit you on the jack, Seawitz.

ᴆᴆ

Usually dove eyed, yet
Sometimes he'd come in looking like he might
rob you.

This engine hates to idle,
Dusk bringing up the rear,
full sail in a littoral privateer.

Tap dancer,
Box bungalow.
I cast a skull on the prow,
His hull split the clouds.

Study a second,
Tropical depression Harrison.

S'mores, sure,
speak softly but carry a big bowie.

One of these days Ayèlet,
bam straight to moon.

A brigand and
a thatcher's daughter
would kiss.

Extravagantly foxy

Weilerswist,
Frederick of the Empty Pockets.

Daimyo wind rifle
To The Ten Thousand Year Bell.
Carcel burner, the Doubloon,
argand lamp.

ᗡᗞ

Care smile, cleft stick
transposition of animal habits
to human consciousness
is humorous.

3 birthday balloons in a tree,
a cluster of red balloons
dead in the gutter.

Fretsaw,
Oders of ear cutter,
snake doctor.

Will my anger or adoration
resound through the ages?

Everyone shopping carts and duels,
Poets foraging for food and contact,
I'll rock a clutch black beret all damn day.

Ladies of color,
woman of the night.

Two
Solariums

Suddenly, I heard something sweet.
I shifted attention from my eyes to my ears.

Think I got everything good.

What's an itch on a lodestar,
For the last twenty years
I've been working on the railroad.

Sleeping brigand,
Slithering motion
Moment of venom

All is fluid
Before it is
Rock.

All of it behind you now,
Almost as if it never happened.

That's poetry,
Or at least it's vertex.

∞

A spider, a scarecrow,
A locomotive of a man
Bearing down the track.

What if suddenly you had great difficulty
distinguishing fantasy from reality?

So many bright systems feed into our obscure world,
You should feel like a hunted wizard.

Cowry courts.
A swirl of flamenco,
Jugglers of sound.

She rubs her face against the music.
I want to write a poem
that crawls into the walls of your cervix.

Epilogue.
Don't mind me if I do,
A word bank.

How many Bangalorians
to build four Deloreans?
Find me another rhyme.

A funny line,
A timeless time,
dwindling duende.

The ice is still cold
In my dove's old glass.

I'm going to hit the books
At midnight in the stacks.

Like the last peanut butter cup,
Thoroughly
Mellifluous.

I may have stepped out a comic
clavicle attack wax
slum musketeer

bait switch

The I want to be with you
for the rest of my days,

smoke in the nook
on my way down Broadway.

Statue
cut by snowstorm.

Prosperous.
Put the needle
on the record

harvestman,
you may say firebrand,
I say flammard.
Deplete our
mountain oysters
upon this jagged shard.

It's a bad habit, I will admit
it can be quite fun at times.

Chaturanga,
Blocking the elephant's eye
In rogue-variants.

En passant,
sticks on the floor of the Styx,
where he belongs.

My cries and laughs
now sound the same.

Sundials in an inlet,
Device of prophecy.
Windfall, watershed,
Vigorous guile.

Would be alone,
fancied a dance.

Backflip,

Constable Brandon Flammard
ordered the Special Bento Box.

Open Flue

How did you do it,
Vincent!

Contradistinction.
Old soldier, sore and sick,
I wrote it on the cloud.

Ribbon fell free
in the vanishing passage.

I want to be where the action is,
Curbs eat people.
I know better.

The solo kettle.
Today's lesson—memory.
Teach me something great.

These are the last words of my grandfather—
I remember, I remember.

Relax while you can.
I am someone, indeed.
The dead have read my poems
and are pleased.

ᗡᗡ

Today I sent my dove a message.
Yesterday she received it.

Implausible fantasy.

Quicksand.
Every clock tower needs a hunchback.

Bikehouse. Building
made of guy. House
made of bike.

Tighten your two-leathers.
Join me for a joint.

Something in the cliffs, Seawitz?
Snakes in misty derangement.

Tufty cotton candy,
Ephemeral duende.

I don't use a baton.
I eat it directly from the machine,
like a real man.

A Stanza is a Splendid Device

Do not be alarmed,
This is just
A bump in the park.

All systems go,
My bitter
Puppetmaster.

Truth
Clarifies
Dark.

Corn will never
Be sugar.

How you fish
Like a fly
In bright blots of sea.

He is warm in sky,
Glazed celadon
With sixty mild Novembers.

Seasons flicker
By on the coffee-stained
Nickelodeon.

Breakfast
Is served.
Mandarins.

Mandolins.
A fenceless façade

softens senseless.

I used to wipe off the ink,
No matter how it felt.
Now I just miss my wild memoir.

Signed Below

This is your assignment,
you have two score hour.

Do you have wooden stakes
to dismantle an empire?

It will be by groove of dagger,
by wine of blood & iron.

There is a rogue passage
to the palace promenade.

You will know the moment
to strike from a balustrade,

fervent serpent of the last gasp,
depart this duke with a cold rasp.

The Man for the Job

He is within a macabre cloak
That swiftly caresses his boot,
Out of nether he steps to the world,
Wearing his human suit.

Deramoor Glume
A name that brings quiet before the form.
His eyes a harpooning grey,
Dread and forlorn.

He draws contract with digits of artifice,
Black beneath his hood murmurs to acquiesce.
A lone fingertip procures inked insignia
And he begins his pernicious descent,

Like a plague among men,
Deramoor Glume
Wakes county from gilded dream
Into dusky doom.

The lights flicker in furthest room.
Victim looks round with unclean frown.
Like nightmarish spins of the loom,
Deramoor Glume
Lets his blood slither down.

Oubliette

My home is
hissing radiators
and hypnagogic states,

Maple marshmallows,
Nitric mudflats
and thunder wyverns.

Rockwool and vermiculite,
I would live in an endless autumn.

Unluckiest baron,
Lost to the halcyon glaze of a chocolate chip
ice cream sandwich.

Can't skip out on a classic.
It all swivels into place.

And so it goes
in a manner you will regret
like floundering fall
of the goliath's footstep,

So like the flight of a dove,
like a gentle whiskey rub—

Taproot. Sphagnum,
Sweet winds of eternal autumn.

ᴆ

Nebulized,

Ash on the tongue
Ash on the lip,

Cash on the roulette
That goes click-click... Click.

Chicken wings and onion rings.

North a valley atop a mountain
at the end of a red dirt road
is my home.

I've heard it's hip to be square.
Kind is the new cool.

Mildly,
Bronzed washers
Togue the cade,
Surf the curb.

ᴏᴐ

Periderm mimer wilt goo,

Towering judge,
irate brackish
phony lathwork.

Aeneous, aureate

Clean soul,
bread alone.

Parts of the car take purchase,
Jungle hijinks japes jinkies.

Eerie triumph,

Eyes like babies in double oubliettes.

ᴏᴐ

Scorched to a cancerous crisp
Around every corner,

rubble of my room,
situational dub.

I work my
Magic and that's that,

With a wink, a snap,
A tip of the hat.

Gear and grit,
Hip witch.

Anywise violas,
likewise mirk umiaq.

These cleopatras
on my relaxing rush to class.

ᴆᴆ

dope chess,
Comestibles in the kitchen
combust.

The bag is packed.
Will you stay awake
so we don't end up in Jamaica?
My prints are on file.

Buckbean and nutwood,
Oxtails.

Hedgepig zyme destine clandestine

JÖKULHAUPS

There is Samantha
Amid bats in the underground,
Between the rosebush and tidepool
Prying the copper out a rotor.

ᴆᴆ

Splendid array,
Tug of war with a tiger.
Goblets of ire, punchbowl of cash

Wizard of Oz, Seawitz.
Monsignor brilliant but remote,

Dreams crumble to dust
in a deck of smokes.

Credulous cartwheels.
You got this God,
Bring my sheep out to pasture
Measure for
Measure.

I think this country has had enough
of us poets

like something out of a motel
in north Florida coral pink.

Residual visuals,
Peeshy.
Fireside chat with a Cleopatra cat.

When it all comes up roses
When it all goes pear,

Tread road where lupin poses
Dine on the air.

Running road of noses,
Huffing down.
Dicey, icy and dodgy,
Go by in blink of doleful eye.

Residual visuals,
Carapace of the scarab.
Tolling of haunted towers.

Hold your horsepower,
I'm charging
To liftoff.

The mind is a storm of time and information.

Diacritical timescales,
Butterflied bags, gemmed and begrimed reliquaries.

Bungee cable,
Turning Dijon grey
In the oubliette.

Rage puppet.
Call it quids on the kettle.

A synopsis of the synapse.
Wild talkies,
Puzzle of flesh.

Today, a trap.
Tomorrow, brown bread.

Rolling round my ripples of red,
You're drawing cards but you should be dead.

Self-portrait holding a pom
Afore all volumes of the Bavli,
When I was a shining bright American lad.

Adaptations,

Five of seven eyelids flicker
in slaked acacias.

I used to take a black jaguar to town.
Now, I ride a rusted cycle to work.
Wipe that grin of your smirk,
Behind me into the batty underground.

Dry Interior

The needle lifts,
The record begins to spin.
The light is red,
I grin,
Become the guy who listens
to China Cat Sunflower
at 4 In the morning.

The record rolls to a stop—
Welcome to my workshop.

I wish I could say arabesques—
Just don't slip
In the jagged mirror.

A visionary
With a white hat
Comes much credibility.

A man of many clocks,
Signaling spiraling need.

I want to write something that chucks you in its trunk.

Take one last sit on Mirage Chair,
Even though its barely there.
One fast look at the Pendelton,
A quick glance at the Kawasaki,
Whiff a note of the tallow & dandelion
and walk where the path is a little less rocky.

Hinterland Harvest

Cherry tomatoes
Flush from harvest,
Plump as plumstones
And just as marvelous.

Like a glide down an old lane.
Tea with your forebears in the pane,
Friendly in sugar stalks.
Like a blood moon against a porcelain backdrop,
This piece is a dash of temporal dissonance
In your Bloody Mary.

Arms Poetica

Poetry as an entrance,
A poem will entrance.

Poetry like lightning on the green.
Poetry, your speck of antimatter
Suspended perfectly,
in a magnetic bottle
where if the slightest thing's awry,
The whole bloody world just might
                    ᗡᗡ
Poetry like a drumroll drops
as the bass kicks,
Poetry like the lock's
inaudible click.

I could do this all day.
One might say,
I've read a world about wordplay,
And I'd rather invoke an essence
than lilt defenseless.

A bleak heart poetica,
Let it ring against eternity—
Poetry as poetry,
Swirly in a snowy tree.

Well, hornets like the faucet flows,
If it is not a rhyme,
There is no time.
And I duly suppose
Despite your perception,
There is no substitution
For conviction.

Tonight I Suppose

Dinner for two at The Press Gang,
Seawitz,

and drinks afterward at
Cherry Like Neon

Sign illuminating.

I could perform this jig again,
I can be your unborn friend.

My impresario's imposters
and every ruddy lady I know
on blurry joywalks through sparkling snow.

Followed my shadow
to the shabby ashery,
then we brushed past,
whetting the tool via random knife.

Draw, my dear.
Kick it into high gear,
Eloquence & beauty align.

What's the blush? Why put up a blight?
Eternity will be a lush, plush push of lux light.

Splinter

I dropped a grape into the underbrush,
which is a big deal for little things that tick.

Final splint,
Splicing time.
Dangerous license.

From lycanthropy to the gallows.
Heat of exhaust on my leg,
This holy husk.

ᙠᙔ

Therianthropy, professed ability,
a conjectural dervish upon lacquer.

Keep plucking at the out of
tune harpsichord,
perhaps you're driving at something,
Eating cotton candy in bed like a mad Roman.

Classic thirsty,
Write it onto solid state chocolate.
I've seen enough,
Moreau's madness, monsters manufactured.

You do not want the sear of my words,
you do not wish an anathema upon your head.
There are engines which emit time,
Things seem to rot around you.

Thalassicola and protoconch,
Phoenician purple, *tekhelet* blues.
Leuco state to lamitor flow,
Indigotin dragoons.

A standard-winged nightjar
Alights on a blue milk mushroom

She looked so cute in that butterfly costume,
My life laid out on mycelia of a monsoon.

Avicultural,
common bronzewing in pendulous weather.
There are dark portals and air charters
in which I down mint juleps.

Samantha's mini pepper box,
Poetry professor popped a portal.

It is algid, it is dire, a dirge—
A flip of coin, a little softshoe,
Whirling a cello
        in the slant and flapwork.

It is a long time between drinks
You're alive, Seawitz!
Where to next? Asleep at the heel?

Chilly Canning,
Crash din the pan.

Tellurian tones,
I could use a pancake.
Bizarre midnight band session,
I won't keep you on a night this cold.

It's worth fjording.
When did poets
Become pirates?

Psych experiment for cash.
At the end of the A
A flip.

Pass a snarl back to the guy who just bit your heel,
Demand they hold the slicing door.

Watch fast clock slow.
I have contemplated all of the elements
and have chosen a mix of fire, shadow & æther.

Carcel prime,
Smell of N.Y.,
Time capsule
A tumor upon the evening.

Pawns,
A vernacular of acronyms.

Great steppings
Past 2boots once in a blue moon.

Reliquary. Wheelock. Carbine.
Sumptuaries. Fainting goat feints
onto fainting lounge.
Nectarivore,
Stomp stampede plague of beasts.
Nacatl coatl camel koalas.

Rainy weepy weak,
A rapt weep lick.
Jive & vex in the grainy nautical
Unbegotten waif
of the Bernoulli effect,
Only plume this side of Roma.

Wing smack,
Disturbances in the ionosphere.
Baby hydra
Flashback to evergreens
Peradventure,
Jade to jute to joust in jungle japes
Prion prawns.

As if my star were rising again,
A Faustian bargain,
Bangle and targes.
Plain derangement.

Qualms barge,
Great poems rewritten.

The lilied wha watering
Rumbling umbras of the violoncello,

A pannier tie-in
Stipulates the lathiest sum.

Horizon cindered thin.
You like when tinder
is under your skin.

Greasy ass napkin,
The driest spit.
All right, that's it.

Icy Road

What is an icy, ivied road?
Leap from rafter to girder,
Dreamy demon herder.

Kentucky death trip.
Can I snag one of those, Seawitz?
Mountain mix,
Safe drops from sky.

Keep hands on the toad and balls on the wheel,
Sun on tarmac. Angel, beetle, petrol power wheedle
celeritous deceleration
Freudian cascade.

Will someone walk up the stairs out of my memory?

Surely such a day will come again.
This is how a man carves out his chicken,
bread & bananas.

It is dank and orange on the road
When the purple track ascends its climax.
Gliding forward,
An agent untoward.

Sleipnir, Sleipnir & Fenrir
in the ferns,
A thing pernicious beyond the corner.

Why is seared muscle so tasty?
What about when a child confronts his first
failing business?

Retreat to my dominion
Need juice in a glass,
Crying and hitting a rat.

Come near my good ear
caught in the reverb,
Shut the tape deck.

Waypoint monsoon
ignition of cognition.
Perfection of the mood.

Dust storm wedding
on walnut coast.

Ahead of you now
hopscotching through a conspiracy of ravens.

ꝏ

Brilliant development,
There is very limited proof of my greatness, perhaps
just tonight's run,

South side of the sky.
A door in the dark
Where rancor recurs.

Let's jet,
Out of gas.
Botulism, slipjacks.

Now I am in the left lane,
Corners dripping with poison.
Something insidious around the bend.

When the spark hits the gas

EYE OF THE POEM,

Citizen of the stratosphere.
Sympatico blizzard

Gristlediscs,

In the cracked enoteca—
Man without a loop,
Pleasant view of cemetery.

See things in terms of eternity,
Fulguritic thundersnow
petrified thunderbolt,
mile deep clouds and rainbands.

Wreath of aurora
æther turning,
Don't you love
when birds are burning?

A man of many expenses.
A far cry from the Dunhills of earlier.

Chameleon serpent,
Scrawl in black callbox
with properties.

Wales to the west.
Rip the vert a time or two,
read a leaf of Magician's Nephew.
Ask what makes a great tale,
and I will tell you.

Harrisoned without a hand,

Just a human on a horse.

One day I lope
To Isle d'Hot,

Obsidian fields,
Lamplit byways
To seaside highways.
Light is healthy.

Music that could turn
A wasp friendly.

Seawitz snapped his pipe.
I saw the coattails of an angel.

Jetsam & Koi

They don't make them like this anymore.

I am probably destined to die
an early and tragic death,
Growing lonely and autophobic
In a system with an absence of logic,
Tumbleweed,
Mummified mermaid
& dusty automata

Off Heathcliff Harbor,
Off Cardiff,
Annapolis,
rustic charm.

Bright cliffs, Seawitz.
A waltz through Amberwald
to Whitesteppe.

Who knows why we do what we do,
but we certainly do it.

Standing stones, trilobite earthworks.
Trilithons, Salisbury church clock.

A ghost down
In rotten borough,
A bit, a part, a piece.

A swan and pom
in the bunch of grapes.

Brandon's back.

Shooting scar.
I was zooted before,
But now I am lit.

You may find this amusing
On my porch there is a spider
that smokes and listens to Bowie.

Middling movement,
Watershed wavelength,
Crescendoing career.

A beveled edge
in flagstones of the back nine.

Dimeaholics,
tap your deck to the dash
of an $800 car.

Spider mummified wasp,
What is the blessing for sin bathing?

Buckets of bilge.
Boys,
The range is closed.

A bank of a man,
I'm running for *gubernator*.

In my dream last night I had a man o' war.
Then we all rode
to the laundromat,
Then there was a shakedown
and I woke because you called me.

It was an allusion.
Manna fades at
End of phases

A crayon fell from the painting.
Fads populate culture
Then are fading,
Except perhaps certain musicians
Play forever.

Pumpkin spice coffee cake,
My thirst is never-ending.
I don't want to go back to that den of shit.

I'm not really a grape guy,
I don't like raisins.
They are zombie grapes.

Something about smoking on a rollercoaster
Just screams the American dream.

Poplar hall, Seawitz.
Tsafon's last feather.

Jade jacarandas,
The weepy cherry past.
Tomorrow's sack bought today.
Cut the grass,

I should get a snake.
Loser chooses, recycle.
Sickles tickle
Another hand of manaspades,
Another twilight magic game.

Throw down my keys from the magic table.

Conversating in the rye
Covers satin ticking
Doves the way to dover.

Am I an adapting automaton,
Kissing a latrine
and nursing a jellyfish
in a dream?

Could've died
Or worse,
Gotten pulled over.

A requisite for being a poet is being broke
and having no prospects.
We do it for the glory?

Thirsting,
Concerted effort.
Marijuana revivals.

On the draw, on the move,
Castle stalker.
Sorry ride, proud walk.

Strawberry pesticides
Delicious pernicious,
Tear sandwich.

Zombie tapes,
Inception hearken.

Fly into my aerie,

A place where I can look out into the great nothing.
F—

Bricktower skypass,
a pleasant view of the end of the map,
the ravine, the watchtower, the box in the pine.

Tendency is to burn evenly.
Cessna Harrison,
It is a long time between treats.

Smoke through the bland.
I was lit before,
Now I am lifted.

Pearly gate, climb in the numb womb.

The thieves: leave it.
He's going to need it.

Wheel and deal.
Benson ride, Dunhill drive.
Long day of lazing alive.

Each day is looking wetter than the last.
Sunbaked turtles,
Me of little faith.

Smokey bones,
Sleeve that, I'll stash this, back in a bit
somewhat remiss.

Cavernous hair,
I had you at have three.
Dragon feeds on emerald.

Found a little church,
Dearest in the parish.
Had a bit of mirth,
Daring in the marsh.

Can I pay in karma?

This one cloud is so like the Lord.
Boys,
The range is closed.

You do not eat sunflower seeds
At the mulch,
Man with twenty-one empresses.

You got nice action.
Call it pax and I'll come back,
Unlucky baron.

Post-pastrianism.
Something about this Englishman is different.
Worst things happen at sea.

Jetsam and koi,
I am a federation Jew.
Enlightenment missed these parts.
Stop violating the Torah all over me
under the porte-cochère of a cashmere port.

Itchy junkie,
Have a toasted coconut doughnut.
Send a nice card and a jar of blood.
Alan was my Sunday school teacher's name.

Cricketsong Canter

I'll always be a Plant City lad at heart.
The juiciest detail in the skypad,
My porch is a honky-tonk.

Gum in the sun,
Train ordinances
& churchside burgeoning.

Break your dash,
if you want it so badly.
Two words: New York.

Another day,
another deck of Dunhills.
Soak an el with Derek on the torch.

Teapies,
Humming mums
Stoop in the moot.

Tragic magic—
A rainbow issuing of a well

Twirl the lacquer,
or we shall just listen to crickets.

Mull drift.
Pull up to the big oak.
Taste the world standard in flavor.

Maintain the machine,
Fume in the boiler room.
Steams wheeze to crisis,

then exhume.

How fast will you speed,
how quick will you bleed
when avarice reaves
your sunwashed steed?

Last damp match,
the last Dunhill.
For a final time
fill my poppy still.

She bungles overt
Simmering with charisma.
Fuddles on the verge,
Spewing plasmatic blue miasma.

Waxy Road

Scaena prima.
The wheels are squelching
On a silken caravan.

It begins with honey,
And distends in mellified man.

What is the salt
of waxen vortex?
Liberty from the rift
of temporal tempests.

Anthropodermic bibliopegy,
Beside powdered rhino horn.

Bile of moon bears
harvested via fistulae.

You may as well bite the piranha.
From lion mind to high arcana,
It is all a fata morgana.

A flashing sear brimming up deep,
clash of centuries beneath the feet.

The chaining grip of eternal sleep,
Scarabic battalion in the under creep.

Icaric wings will uncurl & span—
To an unction merchant's land,
to mummified fumes of sand.

It begins with honey

And ends in mellified man.

Slithering Bosk

Some thing begins to crawl.
This poem begins to begin.
In a brown car in the badlands,
This could be the final trip downtown.

What shall unfold in this disfiguring cold?

Night cools sand dunes
Under a carousel of a charade.
The cornsnake watches, eye macabre,
As his hands rescind & vanish.
What dreams does sin banish!

Black writhing all nooks of ruddy parish.
Blighted tithing upon the fair & bloody fairest.
Petrified lightning forms a fare up garish crest,
I sink into wet dross
& dream's drowsy arrest.

Tightrope Travails

The string snaps taut,
ankle caught in the mirror.
Polyphasic sleeper,
Focus in rising heat shimmer.

Don't look down, don't drop
to Sheol, in grief.
See clouds in a dewdrop
on a cindering leaf.

A wistful brook back
to the ichor, the wax.
Juggling wealth, poetry and chocolate
in a balancing act.

Skanking daggering waltz,
Ink, eyedrops and quicksilver pits.

Kettledrums
of cascade grove, Seawitz.

Shore Road.
The bog's edge.
A slithering pulse,
A smoke in time.

I hark to your hyalopterous loquacity,
bacciferous bride of mayapple and ghostberry,

Cinnamon mill in the moonstrip mirror.
Civilization sits on a sinking pillar.

Sleight of the Seraph

I sank to my nadir
as tendrils of the quickthorn.
Garlanded in magma, wreathed in miasma,
Alongside my sour corpus' torn form
Bawdy Balance weighs out blue plasma.

Husked to ethereal plane of swirling luminous downs,
What'll I inscribe? Misty track through future glades
of Olympia, counting my viscount of debutante days?

A pink-toed antilles responds to lovely feeling,
He sews a web over a corner of my ceiling.
The cornsnake is not pleased, is ailing.
Three domains slowly reclaim my bungalow.

Demonic destiny knocks thrice and hard,
So a paltry waltz off this jagged shard.
Sealed in a reliquary, amid barks of the bestiary.

Downhill Dally

After I am sealed in the armoire of psychedelia,
And have crossed into the coffiny aftergames,
I want my corpse shot into space.

Park in the atmosphere.
My wife has fire in her eye
And a harpstring in her hand.

Kinah for the Lord,
Kavod in the sand.

I'll be passing through a strobic cloud of nerve gas,
Jeremiah of these waters,
Hashing through compositions of the past, upheaval
of sunken orders.

The oders implore their swarms
bower orphic descent.
Sharp bugles raise the alarm,
as I zither into the vent.

Now is a genial time to relate that Lewis line,
Suppose it was on no signposts,
and a road to Sheol paved with brick of oblivion.

Love so uninspiring,
Despair worthy writing.
I'm losing my mind to scarabs & cold.

I wish I didn't know
any of the people I know.
You wish you were Brigitte Bardot.

Backwater Barreling

The idea of sacred time.
Arrester wires a-go,
So may I sit here & feed my animal soul?

Be it liquor run from Havana,
Or tracks through parish in black snow,
In gliding ghostberry bramble peek fawn & foal.

I'll let you ask the Q,
It is not late enough.
Not for this dim doing,
In the dark of the bluff.

Lighthouse spirals down to crust,
Waxing in mirrory flux.
All my things in a few rucks,
Weaving diamonds from the dust.

My Dude's Doppelgänger

This was made for the generations,
Like the creamiest malt.

From the cherry nipping apparatus
Can you see the bugling brasses,
Prancing viola playing lasses,
Chimneyswept vesper flashes?
Is that really me? Could it be my fault?

To the ashes,
Topaz eyelashes.
Only diamonds of time
Well hope to exalt.

Smell is fell.
Ahh, nothing
and maybe a bit of soap.

The gearing vault.
An engine of a man
Ought never grind to total halt,

Until his ash in the pan
filters into my salt.

Tesla's Final Project

The power of suggestion.
Chipped red lead chess set,
A man is his fashion of expression.

Humanity plants the seed,
Technology grows the tree.
Hooked on that gator in the water.

Reset emulation.
Psychotherapist philosophile,
Know that doves kiss all the while
In dead links to living poetry.

Bad Hebrew of Illyria,
Pidgin Aramaic Ostia,
Unspeakable, unsigned Petra.
Sensible vehicle America.

Third verse of delicious tangents.
The morbid truth,
Misting pheasants.

The Nudist Café

I have no delusions as to what time it is
as I sip palmer and cross a bony bridge.
Can the whole hood hear me hacking,
will town be drowned in a brook of my bile?

You will not divine or soothsay,
you will erase superstition.
Ever had a fortune resting on a J?
Shock in tropics, inotropic oocyte.

The wind is red in any fade,
Choked up luck under tree trunk shade.
The river white with manna glaze,
Mix the sky into lemonade.

They look like you're about to feel.
Do a J at your J,
head to the record J then back to my J for more J's.

Iniquities of antiquities.
Pour my inadequacies on the pavement
In a horny mourn.
Daily discomfort in the deciduous deserts.

Hey all bright monster thing,
Push your baby in a rusty swing,
Through dead diptychs of the historical perspective.

A dream is like a coaster.
Nasilization.
Cinnamon bread, waiting for the kettle to kick.

That feather feeling

Infundibiliform.
The ratchet of the damned.

Could it be Caroline?
A name that sends cold shivers down my spine,
Inscribed in the sweet nectars and crystals I imbibe.

Unusual lights, faded dialogue.
Back alley of black poui,
midnight joy lounge through a nudist café.

Come to Pass

Chromatology,
Stomata of auras.
Flickering chromatograph.

Provenance perturbs perception.
I didn't know they were from Sweden.

You should wing this,
before it goes out
to the source of the sound.

Clutching a bo,
Hiding a sai,
Fifty bricks in the bank.

Not a brand I know and love.
Can't have a browse and a bev,
In aisles of toy guillotine witchcraft.
Costumes & coats, Seawitz.

Over before I've begun to race.
The optics click into place.

A wandering eye tracking the soar.
Is life so very different from a dream,
In a back alley peepshow?

We see what we wish to see.
What is clear to you
Can be verily cloudy.

If I can do it I'll duet,
But you ought not post to the internet.

A poet first
in an American second.
French-made,
South stitched too tight to speak.

What is with tonight?
Offer catnip to a rabid flying fox.
I gnashed a Nazi swing pipe in half.

Sizzle

Waffle on the hibachi,
A twist of Twain
the sinking tile.
Perusing the mega-file.

Pirouetting paraphilia,
whoosh of another man.
The ghastly guile
& gliding argyle.

Ah well, all trolleys clink to a stop.
My mane is a butcher shop,
you would not believe how much red meat.

One of those mornings well-tailored
for scrubbing up the oil of my failure…

There is a lake
where there was a welder.

Winging wax
fizzles with the flax.

Jordan Fording

I dig your noose ends, Jordan Hewson,
In shadow of illusion, when is golden?

I've sunk to a drone in her nest.
Punt him out a window with haymaker to chest.

Smoke your pen and write in ash,
Dip your hand in the honeypot.

Smoke in the attic and enjoy coconuts on the lawn
in a tangerine Singaporean dawn.

I've begun to sweat in my sleep.
Carve a door into a tree
and pass through it out of being.

How long was I alone in my solarium?
Pinball and poetry are one.

Indulge like a Roman peasant.
Sentence of my essence
Robs essence of this sentence.
A light speed fox makes a hell of a present.

Lunar Larking

Salutes of the flute.
Asbestos platoon through the jungle.
Castrophony, animism, tainted cannabis.

Fighting stance,
out wicks the lamp.
Guerilla ringleader of faux festivals.

Imagination runs mild.
Wound cauterizes beneath gauzy spool,
You take this fair weather balloon for a fool.

Would've in the Marrakesh.
A mewling ditch.
Lightning stance—

Amid sham, the scheme,
The tomfoolery,
The jewelry-framed scene
of razor-laced wooery…

Just take some shake
for the hard road ahead.
Follow the thorny crowberries,
skirr my ferry through murky hollow.

At unease whenever there is a thin curtain
between me and last breath.

Lesser rorqual,
Giant squid and foxhounds
in swirling turquoise.

The gondola is sinking.
What tore out your wing
while we were lunar larking?

Riding stance.
Slow at first,
And then avalanche.

ᗡᗡ

Confiscate a caravel,
Barrel of elderflower wax.
Rogue-variants, thimblerig
& swiftest legerdemain.

Jet-fueled gent.
A wing, a fang,
A lance of bats,
A missile of bitch.

Flowing stance, spiraling sand,
Leaking out into cold charged shadow.

Rocking the thin line between dreadful and sublime,
Tipping my cap in fateful joywalks through time.

The roost is over,
It's on the runway.
We've reached decision speed.

Liftoff has arrived.
Exodus is migration.
I want to go to the highest *sphirot*.

I've found what I was looking for,
thrice over.
A walk, a pipe, a nap

all that is left.

There comes a time
When a man must tie his shoe and step.
In dusky breath,
He will become one with a woolen bed.

Razor-Leaved Clover

Scaena ultima.

Water warm,
Sailing half-mast,
I steer down a portal
Into the past.

Lies lie like a veil,
Surrounding truth as mist.
This veil pure doth derail,
These lies covet secret tryst.

Hidden beauty,
Thoughtless eye.
Countless stares of love deprived,
I present my soul untrue,
All my gifts unto you.

The evening sky,
It tells me lots
About virtue and truth
Discard and lost.

Glassy eye and alone,
I love you like waves love the shore.
Pulsing, constant and infinite,
Pounding resonance through swirly core.

Wide eye and in despair,
I feel ancient days as quick moments ago,
Crimson beams of light
Let loose to flow.

When I express with written word
It seems conspired mistake.
An unreal cage
Of bass writhing out a lake.

Laura, suffice it to say,
You shall know nothing but undying passion.
Even whilst we part,
Discrete of life's grand flashes.

My heart aflame with tar of regret,
Distress over time that never occurred.
My veins are valleys brimming with lava,
Wavering peaks singed and blurred.

ꝏ

I am dough in your hands.
Wax trickling down candle side,
Warm and soft.

I am amused my muse,
I could not glean or fuse
Another wary notion from your clenched palm.

A sun rising does not bring
What my heart speaks to sing.
Shape me shifted
Into your desire,
Play me like golden lyre.

I am here in the battered depot,
So withhold no fear.
Ahead a hasty shield,
Bread from temporal soil.
Close your eye and begin to see
One can dream when there is no sleep.

I am a slipstream of an idea
Hollowing down the truth.
One last untold galleria
Of lonely aging in vermouth.

Pillar of Cloud

I come to crossroad
Signs loaded with misgivings.
I swing the wheel
In the way of appeal.

On a voyage to the pyramids
In a land of dragons and pariahs,
Heroes and false messiahs,
A dimension is apparent
On the petals of a bloom.

I'm fading
And the sky tells me
That it is beyond the time.
The sky tells me
At yours & mine.

The silver horses round the stable
Are idling for sun on pine,
And blowing winds in starry fables
All gallant in a line.

Bronze is my heart
But gold is my doubt.
I cannot wait,
Urge strikes me now.

Steal shape, my desires,
No matter what transpires.
In a locale nestled within a spire
I combust to ashen fire.

I touch a volatile nexus

Captured in a glyph,
And from underneath
A true myth unveiled.

∞

There is no why,
There is no how,
There is only here
And only now.

It is passion solidified
Upon the brow,
Only here & only now.

It is my heart rekindled
From murdered doubt,
Only here
And only now.

Chisel your needs in the trunk of a tree
And only then can it be sacredly seen,
What must be rinsed clean
From the black recesses of mind,

Memories of woe
Trailing behind.

Addle & Reprieve

I lay far and deep in my subtle cove
Apprehending an untrustworthy stove
Dicing up clove, mandrake to mangrove,
The murky backdrop to the horizon betrothed.

Show me a slideshow of mountain men, hi ho,
And I will presume under bare bulb glow
To pour clear martini and cobalt maraschino
Accenting the grim manifesto of modern hero.

The cyan skull floating in the glass against the bulb,
In a relative Davey Jones locking hold,
Swims to the surface and dips back again,
with this turtlish maneuver I'm minded of my friends.

The days are long,
The years are short.
My time spent here
will forthwith distort.
Hand in jacket, Napoleon style,
I exit stageplays in mild reconcile.

I suppose it's a poor time to confide,
Azure sky rings a teary eye.

Uptown addle, downtown reprieve,
Cabdrivers wild horses ridden side saddle.
In the midst of hustling I roll up sleeve
Break from clutter bric-a-matched prattle,
Toe suspending bridge & rue what I believe.

A Cordial Demand

It is raining on the land of deliverance,
Saturating the earth, voluminous and smooth,
While in the cities men wind round circumstance
And lyric lullabies softly soothe.

Forsaken lovers remain quiet, alone,
Like dusty old novels with silvery tears.
There is a parade somewhere,
Balloons, drums and trombones,
But it is not here.

Sleeping spires, spin a story
Tell of courage on golden fields.
Of causes to die for, red lips, glory,
Just like in the movie reels.

The glistening villa rooftops hang blankets over hill,
The despaired young clasping onto ancient memory.
Peering over hang plants and ends on the windowsill
Out to beige shoal of sea.

Crammed into a bookshelf
Among tales of yore
The evening sky delve
Into forgotten lore.

To be bound to an ageless night
Is a soul bereft, a harrowing cry.
One woven from crafted delights
When the spirit elects to die.

City Life

Where to begin?
On streets that fade the grin,
And crease deep rucks in face
Flushed with gin.

Where to begin...
In a quiet dismal diner
Crooked in a corner
Where bad eggs, cold bean
Amid stale smoke faeries
Is where I shall begin.

All it would take is a some cheap décor
And an occasional mop de floor,
To make it warn within.
But lo, I must assume,
Its constituents like it grim.

How do I loathe thee?
Cliché me the ways,
Men on avenue
Fallen on dusking days.

Still in shadowed repose.
Is it me, cast in rusty streetlight,
Cornered, night after showy night?

Is it playing softly enough,
Sweet suitemate?

Is it in the dark alley lanes,
Where unspeakable flicks to insane?

In tonks where they forget
Through dancing and cocaine
There are men concealed above
Behind tinted windowpane.

I despise misery brought on
By humid drizzling rain.
Does it make steam rise from pavement?
A testament to the past and passed?

Was it by skating off the old iron bridge,
Or a heart pierced by broken glass?

The creaking beds and chipped wall.
Will first breath ever come call?
It is not of this earth, the cloudy pall
Of suppressed mornings, the sun veiled
By opaque smog.

Will it be starving rats in song?
An homage to depressed longing
For a way out of it all.

A stream of pigeon so like schools of marlin.
A Berkin bag. Thanks for the brew,
And thank You too.

I get on train
It takes me away
But I return
Day to day.

I shall have a lachrymose departure
When I am torn from the truth
To where foggy orchestra arias,

In tune to my wavelength.

Glittery stars shall tell of no sin,
Only to define a dream—
The silver hazy screen within
Throes of ethereal mind.

The Schroeder Shuffle

All along back alleys and side streets of New York
Lamplights flicker on as evening draws to a close
And a vagrant on corner speaks hearted benediction,
Wishing fresh linen clothes, those of glass front rows.
Meanwhile amid darkness, among the fact & fiction,
Frozen in time somewhere in mud, hustle & bustle,
A circle of gents swiftly step the Schroeder Shuffle.

Champagne flute in faint hand tinkles on the floor,
After it is swept, denizens arise from sleep,
Slip to evening wear, hats foregone over wavy locks,
And onto the cobblestone in a tobacco reap,
Heel click ladies like flamingo flock
In one-layer dress with pleated ruffle
To dreamily sway the Schroeder Shuffle.

The year is 1931, the builds are all rough and brick
Brownstones down a block, fine shop round avenue,
Poor & broken squat in diner,
Rich in gilded movie parlor,
The tables are all stained with scotchglass residue.
In dim sheath of the Mercer, couple shares a murmur,
Dusky eye leads her from violet and case of truffle,
Hand-on-waist all tonight, to swing a somber shuffle.

Candyshop Eyes

Candy eyes with a glazed dream
Gazing through insides of me.
Lollipop swirls and cocoa curls
Are the eyes of candyshop girls.

Gumdrop nose with a sugary sheen,
Dulcet, prickly passion of sweet thing,
With tender finger, wash me clean
In checkered candyshop gleam.

Cherish me freshly
In dewdrop flushing
On luscious dawn and eve.
Grasp the wandering belief.

Licorice lips and choco kiss hips
Behind counter cup of paperclips
Lilts the aproned girl from my dream,
Softly singing lullabies in mellifluous theme.

If I Could Play the Saxophone

Since I left that body of mine
I cannot remember the truth all the time.
I forget here I am, I forget who I love,
I'm sailing to seas, lifted above.

When heat runs dry and cold comes on,
And sun hides behind wintry song,
I remember New York, the deathly avenue,
Nightmarish pain I cannot construe.

I am a lonely sprite in the mountains alone,
Snowy delights and a life on icy peak cones,
They are only human and we are much more,
As night creeps gone to three and four.

You make me feel in a way others are not able.
You make my world sunned and stable.
I am befit to drift among the living,
Searching for final embers of spirit.

Supine Reprise

Alone in this world,
Since when is that news,
After all the misgivings
This life has produced?

Turbulent and unforgiving
My time misconstrued,
Yet in mists truly clearing
I discern you.

Keep your enemies closer
And me at arm's length
So I can bathe in your rose scent
And warm in your breath.

In deposed riviera ashen deterrence
Fences in flared airy repentance.
On the lover's offensive, declaring my entrance,
With baited stare tensing and starred sparks pensive.

Glow ever brighter in windblown heath,
Send text and smoke signal
And I my presence bequeath,
Haymaker rattled by your astral gleam.

The supine reprise,
Shaken and stirred.
Behind your eyes I metastasize
Sultrily unfurling curled word.

Onto your berth and into your swirls
I will be the first to answer the trills
That escape your south in murderous duress

Sweeping you under my wing to the nest.

If our tree be burned
We'll switch to the next,
And against all that could be incurred
May pomegranate passion never be suppressed.

Something Else

I'm smoking them like candy
And drinking bilge like its brandy,
Fiery convulsions down the gut.

I'm living in my memories now
Just cloudy glimpses of flutter & wow,
I choke down the past like a starving mutt.

So I'll step to the rusty street
And wisp round people I meet
Like an old graveyard ghost, lantern eye.

I'll torch future days, barroom brawl whiplash
In player piano parlors amid glimmers of the cache,
Looking for a shot, a tune, an end.

I wist it was preacher days,
Cast upon by shady sunrays
In a little villa out in South Bend.

But here in chipped paint wall
Whitewash on bloodstain and all,
I really need a new spot to dig.

Almost a beggar on the toad,
Nearly a small, slimy road.
All my income from thimblerig.

What's the sharp shit on the tongue,
Swallowed dream, or red up the lung?
I wouldn't know the differing.

Mourn for touch of lady I never had,

Be dismal real quiet, sleep real sad.
I couldn't hurt the flaxen-hair so fair.

I'm coughing now, real grisly, real loud,
Scattering dizzily upon the ground.
Please tell me this is misery's nightmare!

It is real. It is as real as you and me.
As real as honey bee in solemn birch tree.
As real as long, hot summer poetry.

Scarlet Wreath Purge

Over the land, a plague in the cold,
Eater of life, drinker of soul,
Drifting through village windows, frayed tales told,
Birthing swarms of scarab in empty porridgebowl.

Slipping in the craggy cairns of old,
It wears the centuries to fine dust.
Over the meadows, the hills, it rolls
Seeking to impart deceitful lust.

In valley tears, a lotus bloom
Petals peel back, onto their backs,
Releasing ash to pollinate sorrowful gloom
Singing of a lingering, smashed pact.

Shadow flits and floats, resting beneath
While is set on the sill
A sharp scarlet wreath,
Prickly poison breeding ill.

A plague in the cold, startle of betrayal,
Lifts from ground, granting final peace
To those caught in its thorny trail
Pierced by a sharp scarlet wreath.

Confidence to Arrogance

Let me tell you
Of my dream
And it shall seem
To blend well
with the curtain.

Setting five-alarms for five in the morning.
What will Wednesday wing?
What's within woman's will?

Shield of Achilles.
A love-set tragedy.
Narrow, zigzaggy poetry.

Oh, you're a real dreamboat,
Out being shady with a sunflower sachet.
Dinner is best served cold,
Rancid ramen and stale taste.

I ate a packet of rotten crisps for breakfast.
I have become a villain.
New York shall drown in flame.

I relate very dearly with this rap.
Down to three fags, my name & an ivy cap.
Well, isn't that kind of that?

Concordant clangs climax,
This joyride has breached impasse.

Contours of a blur.
I wish I could escape the wrists of winter,
tearing depart this mirrory nether.

Lore-Laced Lope

Is there a miracle in vein of the Milky Way?

A whole other act of sweet & savory.
A small town player,
A case of curiosities
& crate of Cadbury.

Licorice allsorts in tender dreams,
A light and an old lager for lunch.

Nothing but binoculars
and a Balkan Sobranje.

ᘉᘈ

You know a well-done production
when a floor model's the last humdrum one.

Creeping kudzu
leaps to thumbdrum.
A lilting lope to cigarette sojourn.

Defer to your discretion
Down a lime-lined hatch
On a gallop of the gorge
track, suit & match.

Sealed amber resin,
You got to be Zen.
Peruse Analects.

Pencil pretty Purim plans.
Lacrimal, the nifty dip—
Quit this carnival of the damned.

Subtle Mint Dusk Drop

Proffered from linty pants pocket
As stern trade embargo,
A capricious reef snorkel for sunken coin cargo.
A face complacent, placid and tacit
Diminutive white ovoid facet.

Exploding with flavor
Or eroding nasty breath
With peppermint life
Or cinnamon menthe.
A subtle mint
Confectioned in factory-reliant
Connecticut settlement.

Cooling padlock of the loin,
Warming thoughts in the mind,
Sparking sweet exhales to come,
Leaving mottled aftertaste behind.

Have a mint, a sit, a light
And hasten on with your life.

www.ingramcontent.com/pod-product-compliance
Lightning Source LLC
Chambersburg PA
CBHW020556030426
42337CB00013B/1107